D1022143

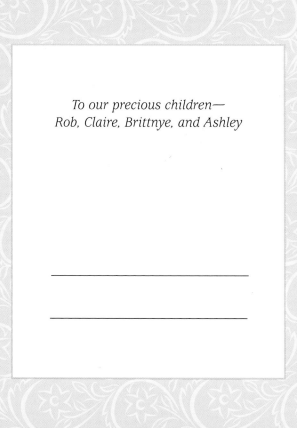

To our precious children—
Rob, Claire, Brittnye, and Ashley

_____

_____

Photo Credits include: Richard Shock/TSI–page 5; Cleo Photography–
page 11; Stephen Simpson/FPG–page 35; Roy Gumpel/TSI–page 40;
From *A Week in the Life of the LCMS*–pages 7 and 29.

Scripture quotations are taken from the HOLY BIBLE, NEW INTERNATIONAL
VERSION®. NIV®. Copyright © 1973, 1978, 1984 by International Bible
Society. Used by permission of Zondervan Publishing House. All rights
reserved.
Copyright © 1999 Concordia Publishing House
3558 S. Jefferson Avenue, St. Louis, MO 63118-3968
Manufactured in China
All rights reserved. No part of this publication may be reproduced, stored
in a retrieval system, or transmitted, in any form or by any means, elec-
tronic, mechanical, photocopying, recording, or otherwise, without the
prior written permission of Concordia Publishing House.

1 2 3 4 5 6 7 8 9 10 08 07 06 05 04 03 02 01 00 99

THE
ABCs
of
CHRISTIAN
GRAND-
PARENTING

Twenty-six ways to love and nurture
your grandchild today and every day

Robert & Debra Bruce

Appreciate
this new creation
—a beautiful grandchild who is
totally a part of you and
also a child of God.

See, I am doing a new thing!
Now it springs up; do you not perceive it?
I am making a way in the desert and
streams in the wasteland.

Isaiah 43:19

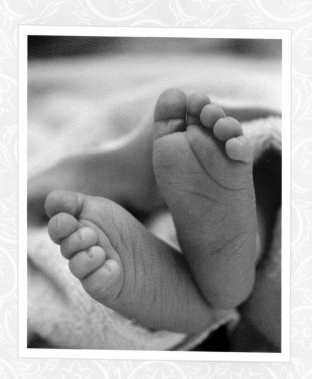

Be impulsive with good deeds.
When you feel a nudge to call,
write a letter, or make something
special for your grandchild,
do it now! The longer you wait
between the thought and the
actual deed, the more likely
you are to procrastinate.

Now listen, you who say, "Today or
tomorrow we will go to this or that city,
spend a year there, carry on business and
make money." Why, you do not even
know what will happen tomorrow.

James 4:13–14

Celebrate
her victories, and empathize
with his defeats. Avoid judging
or making reprimands, but show
the same unconditional love
that God shows to you.

A new command I give you:
Love one another. As I have loved you,
so you must love one another.

John 13:34

Discover

God's creation together
as you take your grandchild
on a nature walk. Talk about how
we are to be good stewards of
God's kingdom on earth.

The earth is the LORD'S and everything
in it, the world, and all who live in it;
for He founded it upon the seas and
established it on the waters.

Psalm 24:1–2

Encourage your grandchild
to keep a spiritual journal,
documenting feelings and thoughts
each day. This journal will be her
special place where she can vent,
contemplate, problem-solve and
dream—without feeling
threatened or intimidated.

How precious to me are Your thoughts,
O God! How vast is the sum of them!
Were I to count them, they would
outnumber the grains of sand.
When I awake, I am still with You.

Psalm 139:17–18

Find time
to go through old photo albums,
sharing pictures of days gone by.
Talk about family resemblances
or personality traits you might
share, and affirm this intimate
connection between you
and your grandchild.

Then we Your people, the sheep of Your
pasture, will praise You forever; from
generation to generation we will
recount Your praise.

Psalm 79:13

Grow
in faith together. Make time
to talk about God's love,
pray aloud, and share
answers to prayer.

For everything that was written in
the past was written to teach us,
so that through endurance and the
encouragement of the Scriptures
we might have hope.

Romans 15:4

Hear

what your grandchild is saying
when he pours his heart out.
Try to remember how it felt
to be his age, and react
reflectively.

My dear brothers, take note of this:
Everyone should be quick to listen,
slow to speak and slow to become angry,
for man's anger does not bring about
the righteous life that God desires.

James 1:19–20

Identify

your grandchild's fears,
and teach her to take leaps
of faith, putting her doubts
aside as God leads the way.

Trust in the LORD and do good;
dwell in the land, and enjoy safe pasture.
Delight yourself in the LORD and He will
give you the desires of your heart.
Commit your way to the LORD;
trust in Him, and He will do this.

Psalm 37:3–5

Jesus'
commandment begins
with our personal witness.
Make time to share your faith,
telling your grandchild of moments
in your life when God became
"real."

In the same way, let your light shine
before men, that they may see your good
deeds and praise your Father in heaven.

Matthew 5:16

Keep
your Bible and daily
devotional guide nearby during
your grandchild's visits. Focus on
Scripture strengths to help
maintain control when
his activities make you
feel tired and harried.

Your Word is a lamp to my feet
and a light for my path.

Psalm 119:105

Laugh
together, and celebrate
your kinship. Wear a smile
on your face as you plan fun
activities to share with
your grandchild.

Rejoice in the Lord always.
I will say it again: Rejoice!

Philippians 4:4

Make
time to tell your grandchild
stories about her mother or father
when they were children, lifting up
their similarities and differences.

Therefore, as we have opportunity, let us
do good to all people, especially to those
who belong to the family of believers.

Galatians 6:10

Nurture

independence and self-sufficiency.
Let your grandchild know that
you think he is a real person, and
allow him to undertake meaningful
projects during his visits.

And God is able to make all grace abound
to you, so that in all things at all times,
having all that you need, you will abound
in every good work.

2 Corinthians 9:8

Openly

solve any disagreements
you may have. Help your
grandchild learn how to share
honest emotions using tact
so feelings are spared and
relationships are strengthened.

Therefore if you are offering your gift at
the altar and there remember that your
brother has something against you,
leave your gift there in front of the altar.
First go and be reconciled to your brother;
then come and offer your gift.

Matthew 5:23–24

give and take when
having discussions, making sure
your grandchild has a chance
to speak her mind and offer
a personal viewpoint.
Encourage her to stand up
for her beliefs.

Therefore encourage one another and build
up each other, just as in fact you are doing.
1 Thessalonians 5:11

Quietly

wait upon the Lord to
give you strength and patience
during a family crisis.

Be still, and know that I am God.

Psalm 46:10

Realize

that your grandchild
will change from visit to visit
as he grows and develops. Hold fast
to the one who never changes—
Jesus Christ, for He is the
same yesterday, today,
and tomorrow.

Jesus Christ is the same yesterday
and today and forever.

Hebrews 13:8

Share agape or Christlike love
with your grandchild—
even when his actions are unlovely.
This self-giving love is filled with
compassion and empathy and seeks
what is best for others.

As God's chosen people, holy and dearly
loved, clothe yourselves with compassion,
kindness, humility, gentleness, and patience.
Bear with each other and forgive whatever
grievances you may have against one
another. Forgive as the Lord forgave you. And
over all these virtues put on love, which binds
them all together in perfect unity.

Colossians 3:12–14

Teach your grandchild to name
her spiritual experiences each day.
Ask her, "What God-pleasing
thoughts did you have today?" Some
examples may be loving thoughts,
thoughts of kindness,
or empathetic thoughts.

Let the Word of Christ dwell in you richly as
you teach and admonish one another with all
wisdom, and as you sing psalms, hymns and
spiritual songs with gratitude in your hearts
to God. And whatever you do, whether in
word or deed, do it all in the name of the
Lord Jesus, giving thanks to God the Father
through Him.   *Colossians 3:16–17*

Uphold

peacemaking in your home,
speaking the truth in love and
serving as a mediator between
grandchildren if there is conflict.

Let us therefore make every effort
to do what leads to peace and
to mutual edification.

Romans 14:19

Value
and respect the rules
and limits your children have set
for their children, and do not
become a stumbling block in
this intimate relationship.

Do nothing out of selfish ambition
or vain conceit, but in humility consider
others better than yourselves.
Philippians 2:3

Watch
your tone of voice.
Instead of communicating in
anger, speak in a manner that
is nonthreatening. Words have the
power to lift up your grandchild
or tear her down, depending
on how they are used.

Do not let any unwholesome talk come out
of your mouths, but only what is helpful for
building others up according to their needs,
that it may benefit those who listen.

Ephesians 4:29

eXplain

to your grandchild
how God's love is always there,
even if she does not feel like it.
Teach your grandchild that God
knows our pain and sorrow,
as well as our hopes and joys,
and has a definite plan
for her life.

And surely I am with you always,
to the very end of the age.

Matthew 28:20

You
may be the best Christian
your grandchild knows,
so watch what you
say and do!

If anyone causes one of these little ones
who believe in Me to sin, it would be
better for him to have a large millstone
hung around his neck and to be drowned
in the depth of the sea.

Matthew 18:6

Zealously

celebrate each grandchild's uniqueness, and spend time with each child individually.

He called a little child and had him stand among them. And He said: "I tell you the truth, unless you change and become like little children, you will never enter the kingdom of heaven. Therefore, whoever humbles himself like this child is the greatest in the kingdom of heaven. And whoever welcomes a little child like this in My name welcomes Me.

Matthew 18:2–5